Sunrise Book

MORAL STORIES 2

SUNRISE

SUNRISE PUBLISHERS

32/33A, Street No. 9, Bhikam Singh Colony, Vishwas Nagar, Shahdara, Delhi - 110032 (India)

Tel : +91-11-71218130, Whatsapp No. : +91-7835078000

E-mail : sunrisepub@gmail.com, export@sunrisepublisher.com

Visit us : www.sunrisepublisher.com

Preface

Stories have always fascinated children, especially the little ones. They get delighted when their grandma or grandpa narrates a story to them. This book is a collection of short stories for children. There is no fixed age group. It can be equally enjoyed by the elderly people. At a young age children should be narrated tales with a moral so that it helps the child in building up his character. Such stories make the child witty, smart and wise.

Stories in this book are true example of worldly wisdom. Each story has been carefully selected keeping the age of a -child in mind. The language is simple enough to capture the heart of a child. Wherever required, the stories are beautifully illustrated with colourful illustrations and lucid language bring life to each story. All the stories in this book are rewritten from famous tales of Panchtantras, Aesop's fables and other legendary tales.

Altogether this-book is a great compilation. Combined efforts of author, illustrators and above all publishers have been a delightful fruit in the form of this book.

Contents

ISBN : 978-81-781313-6-8

Printed by **Tan Prints (India) Pvt. Ltd.**, Village Rohad, Distt. Jhajjar, Haryana

1. The Old Lion

Lion, the king of the jungle, was growing old day by day. His old age was a great problem for him because he could not hunt animals for himself any more. He was no longer able to catch his prey.

But this lion was very cunning. He informed all his friends about his sick health and pretended to be very sick. Whosoever came to meet the sick lion, he would pounce upon it and eat it. Many animals lost their lives until a fox heard about the ill health of the king of the jungle.

"Aah !" cried the king as he saw the fox approaching. "How are you feeling, my lord ?" Asked the fox at a little distance.

"Oh ! I am dying. Only a few days are left of my life. I want to go on pilgrimage in my last days," replied the king. "Yes, you should, my lord ! He said.

"But why are you standing so far ?" Asked the lion "Because, my lord, I have seen all the foot prints going into the cave, but none coming out. And I want to live a long life. So I've decided to keep at a distance and ask about your health," replied the fox and ran away.

Moral : Believe what your eyes see.

2. The Farmer's Teachings

A farmer had four sons. All of them were tall and strong. But they were very lazy and always fighting with each other. The farmer always advised his sons not to fight and start working a bit. But his words had no effect on his sons. They did not listen to their father and quarrelled all the time.

The farmer always thought of how to keep his children together. He wanted his sons to love each other and live in peace. One day his younger brother came to visit him. The farmer discussed his problem at length with him. So he told him a way to keep his sons united. Next morning the farmer called all his sons in his room. He asked them to get a bundle

of sticks. "Sons, I want you to break this bundle without separating the sticks," he said and gave the bundle to his eldest son.

All of them tried one by one but no one could even bend the bundle. "It is a bad condition you've put father. Let us separate the sticks and then you'll see how fast we break all the sticks," said the youngest son. "That is what I want you to know. It is easier to break one stick but very difficult to break a bundle. Similarly, if all of you live separately then anyone can take benefit out of you but if you stay together, tied to each other, with the string of love, no one can ever try to befall you", said the farmer. That day onwards the farmers son never fought with each other.

Moral : United we stand; Divided we fall.

3. The Foolish Lion

Long time ago, in a faraway jungle, a man lived with his daughter. His daughter was a very charming girl. One day a lion was passing by their but when he saw a charming beauty. He, at once, fell in love with her. Day and night passed, but lion kept standing there looking at that girl. Later he decided to tell the girl's father that he wished to marry her. Later one night, the lion reached their and knocked the door. When father opened the door he got terribly scared on seeing a fierce lion but to his surprise the lion said, "Hello Sir ! May I come in ?" "Please tell me why have you come here because my daughter will frightened if she sees you," 'replied the man.

"Sir, I am in love with your daughter and it is my heartiest desire to marry her," he said. The man was terribly afraid. He quickly thought of a plan and replied. "I thank God for sending such a handsome and brave son-in-law for me, but if you love my daughter you will have to clip your nails and teeth off, because she will be scared of them."

So the lion quickly agreed to get his nails and teeth clipped away. When the man removed all his nails and teeth, he shooed the lion away and said, "Sorry my dear, but you do not deserve my daughter. She is a human and you are a beast. Now go away and let us live alone."

Moral : Love is blind.

4. The Two Frogs

Once there lived two frogs named Jantar and Mantar. Jantar and Mantar were brothers, but they were very different from each other. Jantar was very selfish, naughty and rude, whereas Mantar was generous, kind and wise. Their mother always told them to be patience.

One day Jantar and Mantar both went out to play. Suddenly Jantar began to run, when Mantar asked him why was he running he showed him the bowl of milk lying on the table.

So both of them mounted the table. Mantar stopped Jantar to drink milk from the bowl because the bowl was deep and the surface was slippery. But Jantar did not listen. As he bent to drink milk he fell into the bowl. Mantar tried to save his brother but he too fell in the bowl. Now they began to drown.

Mantar asked Jantar to keep moving and trying to reach the top. After trying for a long time Jantar said, "Brother, I think this is the end. I can't try any more so I'll let go. Good bye. But Mantar did not give up. He kept trying to come out of the bowl. After churing a lot, the milk began to harden. Due to heat and constant churning it became stiff. So Mantar could come out easily. He thought, "I wish Jantar was patience. He led us into this problem and killed himself. later he did not even try to save his life." Thinking so he walked back home.

Moral : Be patience and never give up.

5. The Daydreaming Brahmin

Bhola, the Brahmin had gone to another village to perform a Puja. As a reward he got a pot full of rice. After coming back he hung the pot by his bedside and tired as he was, he laid down to rest. Bhola closed his eyes and began to daydream. He thought, "I will not eat even a single grain of this pot, but sell it in the market. Someone will give me 20 rupees for this pot and with those 20 rupees I shall buy two goats." His dream continued "Every day I will feed those goats with fresh, lush green grass and a day will come when they will be fatty. I shall take these plum goats in the market and sell them for 60 rupees.

With those 60 rupees, I shall buy two cows. Then I shall start the milk business. Then I shall have plenty of money and buy some chickens too. Then I will own a big poultry farm." "A rich merchant shall married his daughter to me. Then I shall have 2-3 children. My sons will grow up to be very playful and naughty. One day they shall tease their mother and she will come to me and complain about them. Then I shall pick up a stick and hit them hard." Thinking so he actually picked up a stick lying next to his bed and began to swing it in air. Suddenly the sound of a crash woke him up. He saw that rice was scattered all over the floor. And his dream was over.

Moral : One should think of doing action instead of planning its rewards.

6. The Old Deer

Once upon a time there lived a deer called Raju. Raju was growing old day by day. One day Raju left his family and decided to go away to the mountains where he could live peacefully. So he found a spot where grass was green and air was fresh.

One day some hunters came to the jungle and shot an arrow at Raju. The arrow did not hit him but it passed through its skin. This way he got injured. With difficulty he reached his spot again. Now he had become too weak to move from that place. He wrote a letter to his wife telling her about that accident. So his entire family reached there next

day. When all his relatives heard about his sickness, they too reached that spot to inquire about his health. More the animals, more grass required to feed them. All his family ate the green grass present in that area and then there was no grass left for Raju.

All the other animals could easily move from one place to another in search of food but poor Raju could not. All he could do was to curse the moment when all his relatives came to visit him. At last poor Raju died of hunger and thirst due to the vague attitude of his friends, relatives and family.

Moral : Foolish friends are worst than wise enemies.

7. The Fox and the Wild Boar

Once upon a time there lived a fox. Her name was Nancy. It was always busy playing pranks on others. One day, while Nancy was roaming around, it saw a wild boar. The wild boar was sharpening his tusks. He looked at Nancy and again started sharpening his tusks, as if he was ignoring her. Nancy did not like it. She went to the boar and said, "Hello ! What a bright sunny day. Mr. boar, why don't you come and play with me ?" The boar looked at her angrily and said, "Go away, don't you see I am sharpening my tusks." "But why are you sharpening your

tusks ?" Asked Nancy. "Do you like to fight ?" "No. It is for my protection," said the boar. "But you can sharpen them later, why now?" She asked.

Meanwhile a pack of wolves came there and attacked the wild boar. But somehow, the boar saved his life. Nancy was watching all this. After the fight was over the boar came to Nancy and said, "Do you see why was I sharpening my tusks at that time. Anytime, these wild animals could attack me and kill me if I am not prepared with my sharp tusks."

"One must always be ready with defensive weapons against his enemies", he added and again began to sharpen his tusks. Nancy learnt a good lesson from the wild boar.

Moral : Be prepared for the unpredictable future.

8. The Horse and the Wolf

In a faraway jungle there lived a wolf named Kaliya. Kaliya was a big miser. He never gave even a small bit of his share to anyone, not or even his own children. He used to go out at night, eat the food and come back home. He never thought of feeding his children. Everybody in the jungle knew Kaliya's nature. Kaliya would attend all feasts in the jungle without being invited. Due to this habit his wife and children left him. Now Kaliya was all alone. One day Kaliya did not get anything to eat. So he went to the

oats field. But, unfortunately wolves cannot eat oats. Try as he might but he could not eat even a single one. Kaliya saw that a horse was looking at him. He thought that the horse might make fun of him for not being able to eat oats. "Hello friend ! Look at this ripe field of oats. I've left for you to eat them. So you enjoy them and thank me for that", said Kaliya so the horse had a wholesome meal after having oats he started to walk. Kaliya said, "Hey ! Why didn't you thank me." The horse looked at him and replied," I don't need to thank you for these oats. Had you been so generous to leave oats for me then you would have thought of your children. How do they live ? And you're not that kind to leave food for anyone," saying so the horse walked away.

Moral : Do not Boast off.

9. The Sculpture and God Mercury

A sculptor named Smith lived in a village. Smith was a very gentle man. He made beautiful sculptures which looked real. His sculptures made him quiet rich and popular. Even the Gods had heard about him.

One day God Mercury decided to visit Smith so he disguised as a human and went to Smith's place. There he saw statues of many Gods and Goddesses. He also saw his own sculpture. God Mercury thought that he can know his value in human eye now by asking its price. "How much is god Jupiter's statue for ?" God mercury asked.

"It's only for a gold coin, Sir," replied Smith, "And how much is the price of the statue of Goddess Juno ?" Again God mercury asked "It is for the same price, Sir. I can show you some more beautiful statues. See this one, a beautiful lady", He said pointing towards another statue. "I have just completed this one." He added. "So how much is the statue of God Mercury ?" he asked. "If you buy the sculpture of God Jupiter and Goddess Juno, I shall give it to you for free," replied Smith. God Mercury felt very bad and thought that man does not value him anymore. He stopped working for the good of man and decided never to visit the earth.

Moral : Do not judge yourself, let others do.

10. The Two Friends

Long ago there lived two friends named Mahesh and Dinesh in a village. Mahesh was a very gentle and honest man whereas, Dinesh was a very cunning and dishonest man. One day Mahesh and Dinesh thought of going out of their village to make a fortune. Over a couple of years both Mahesh and Dinesh became rich and decided to go back to their families. Dinesh could think of was only Mahesh's money. On their way back Dinesh asked Mahesh to bury all their money under the old Banyan tree as the way wasn't safe. Mahesh quickly agreed and took some of his money and burried " the rest. That night Dinesh came to the Banyan tree and stole all Mahesh's money.

After a few days Mahesh needed the money so he went to Dinesh's house. Together they went to the Banyan tree but when they did not find the money they went to the judge.

The judge himself could not decide about the matter so Dinesh suggested, "Let us ask the Banyan tree ?" So it was decided that next morning everyone including the judge will go to the Banyan tree. By then Dinesh had asked his father to sit inside the Banyan tree. When the judge asked the Banyan tree "Let us know who is the thief ?" Dinesh's father said, "Mahesh is the thief." The Judge immediately ordered to set the Banyan tree on fire. Dinesh's father came out screaming and begged for his life and said, "Judge, My son Dinesh has taken the money. Please forgive me." Thus, Mahesh got his money and Dinesh got punishment.

Moral : Bad intentions take you nowhere.

11. The Frogs and the Sun

Long time back all the Gods lived on the Earth. They were very nice to all human beings and animals. Only God sun was feared by everyone during the summers and equally loved by them during the winters. All the animals were afraid of God sun but on the contrary, he was very nice to everyone. He used to hide behind a black cloud if everyone was being disturbed by his heat. One day God Sun decided to get married to his beloved. No one was happy on listening to this news. People were sad that the heat would increase. But everyone kept quiet. But the frogs decided to do something about it. All the frogs began to croak aloud. On hearing their voices God Mercury came out of the clouds.

"What is the matter ? Why are you all screaming ?", asked God Mercury. "Oh lord ! Please save us from being killed," said one of the frogs.

"But from what ? Who is going to kill you ? Tell me the matter in detail," asked God Mercury. "The sun is so dangerous even when he is alone but what will happen if he marries another sun ? What will become of us." "Alright. I will tell the sun to keep his wife somewhere else and bless them from your side." So the frogs were satisfied and the newly wedded couple was also blessed by all.

Moral : Trust and love mother nature, for she gives you everything.